Destruction Bay

DESTRUCTION BAY

Lisa D. Chavez

West End Press

Some of these poems have appeared in the following magazines, journals, and collections:

The Americas Review, Calyx, Chiron Review, Exit 13, Floricanto Si! U.S. Latina Poets, Heartland (The Fairbanks Daily News-Miner), Main Street Rag, Mildred, Permafrost, poetryALASKAwomen, Poetry Motel Broadside Series, Sing Heavenly Muse!, The Sky's Own Light, Tsunami.

Thanks to the Jacob K. Javits fellowship program for its support while many of these poems were written.

First edition, January 1999
ISBN: 0-931122-92-9

Book design by Nancy Woodard
Front cover from the painting *Yellow Dog* by Susan Farnham

Distributed by University of New Mexico Press

West End Press • P.O. Box 27334 • Albuquerque, NM 87125

For My Family

Contents

... Because who would believe
the fantastic and terrible story of all of our survival
those who were never meant
to survive?
—Joy Harjo

I

Our Stories

Leave the Window Open at Night

so I can hear the trains
pass by. I listen to them
while you sleep, your body
slack as a half-used bag
of flour. In the morning
these kids reach
for my arms, call me mama.
They have strangers' faces.

When I was a girl
I walked along the tracks
away from this town
full of dust and rusting
hulls of cars.
I thought I'd follow
those trains someday. Instead,
I let you lay me down
in your daddy's old pick-up
truck. I never really wanted it,
but when you looked at me,
you saw someone. That kept me.

Some nights, I slip
the keys from your pocket,
drive down the road
that runs along the track.
I smoke, engine idling, waiting
for the late train.
It comes and I race it,
gas pedal pressed to the floor,
headlights off, darkness
rushing around me. One night

I'll catch that train.
I've been chasing it all my life.

After the Prom

Michael didn't want to go.
A few months shy
of dropping out, he spends
most nights cruising, dealing
"crystal" from his primer grey
Chevelle. I'm a senior—
one last shot at high school
anonymity before the hazy
day-to-day of the life after.
Mom saved her tips from cocktailing;
I bought a second-hand dress
and teased my hair.
Michael rented a tux and wore
a fake diamond earring.
To please me. Then it turns out
to be the same old shit:
Disapproving teachers
tense as we pass, and the school's
stuck-up royalty strutting
towards college—a future
I earned but couldn't afford.
We cut out early.

Driving across town, the Chevelle
shaking at 95, "Freebird" on the radio,
the lights on South Mountain
rising like phantom skyscrapers,
I wish we'd just keep on—
flying through the night
towards death or something
equally dramatic. We don't.
Michael stops for a six-pack

at a place sure to sell it.
Outside, there's a man
leaning against a shopping cart
flooded with blankets. He's so drunk
he sinks to the sidewalk.
He's got a pillow on the bottom
rack, a big feather pillow
like the one on my bed.
That really gets me.
Michael hands him an Old Milwaukee.

Later, I sit in the backseat
of the cooling car, dress rumpled
around me. Michael's pants circle
his knees; he lights a joint,
smoke suspending the air.
And I think of that pillow
bursting in a spray of feathers.
A blinding bouquet.

Goldminer's Wife: Livengood, Alaska

We don't own nothing
outright. Even the house
is built on a claim, not
land we own. Truck payments,
Cat payments, money flowing out
like water from a hose.
Seventy miles from town, there's
nothing here, not even a gas station,
just a scattering of cabins
and the scarred hills.
My old man's been back at the mine
for two weeks now, left me
with nothing to eat
but bread and some jam.
I tell the kids
we're camping; they don't mind.
They pretend they're sluicing;
I hear them laugh
down in the scrub
spruce, and I wonder
what we'll eat tomorrow.

I sit on the porch
sip the last beer
and pray for dust—
not the yellow dust
my man wants to see
at the bottom of the riffle box,
but the white dust we can
buy with it. All I want
is a blizzard of white static,
numbing it all out.

Buried Things

One night in San Francisco
a man I'd only
slept with twice
wrapped his fingers
around my neck
and squeezed.
He let go, then swung
his fist at me casually
in afterthought.
I was standing in the street
in front of a punk-rock club
I stood there and spit my teeth
into the palm of one hand
two small white stones
in a pool of blood and saliva.

I know you are not
like him. But sometimes
I watch you sleep
mouth slightly open
fist curled by
your face like a child
and rage injects
itself into my blood
surges to my hands.
They tremble
above your head.
Poised birds of prey.

The Woman Who Raised Dogs

Most people don't know
about Akitas. Big dogs—fighting
dogs—inscrutable eyes and broad,
bear heads. I raised Dobies
before. They're too high-strung
and nervous, like a woman who's been
beat too much. Akitas are tough,
quiet. I like to see them
in the kennels, a row of spiral tails
curling over broad backs.

Kenji, the pinto male
didn't place last show.
The judge took me aside, said
build up a little bulk,
run him five miles every day.
So I take him out,
watch his muscles snap and pull
as he runs, tongue like a ribbon,
beside the car. I don't get out
much else since Bob left.

Even if I could wash away
the smell of dog, pluck the hairs
from my clothes, what man
would understand? Bob said
if I paid him half as much
attention as those dogs, he'd never
have gone. The week
he left, Kenji got loose, nearly
killed the neighbor's shepherd.
He just flipped that dog over,

went for its throat. I understood.
It's not meanness; they're just eager,
wanting to test their strength
against anything else. Good-natured
killers. Jade, the fawn bitch,
will come into season soon.
Today, she snarls when Kenji approaches,
but tomorrow she may turn her tail
towards him, waiting.
The change is that quick.

Hands

It was his hands
I loved. Big, with long
fingers and blunt
tips. The first time
I felt his hand, hard
calloused but gentle
on my bare breast
I knew I would never
leave. Even after
he lost his gentleness,
when that palm, heavy
as a block of wood
slammed against my jaw—
even then I would not
go. But when I walked
in the bedroom—home early
from my job pressing laundry
down at the White Swan
dry cleaners—when I
walked in and saw him
on top of that red-headed whore
from the beauty shop,
his fingers curled
around her cow tit—when I
saw that, I raised his old
shotgun to my shoulder
and squeezed the trigger.

So it was only
birdshot. But through
the noise and the spray
of lead seeding the air,
I saw fear, saw him
raise and clasp
those hands
as if in prayer.
He won't hold me
back again.

In the Paper, Five Years Later

So you're dead.
Stabbed six times in a fight.
I'm not surprised.
Tell me, as you died,
did the world begin
to darken around the edges,
the way a photograph curls
and blackens in a flame?
That's what I saw, the night
your hands gripped my throat.
I clutched my broken
teeth tight in one hand,
until—forgotten—they dropped
like breadcrumbs, a trail of bone
and blood that would never
lead me home.

I had a knife.
When you grabbed me, I pressed it
just above your belt,
thumb poised above the catch.
The blade shot straight out,
not sideways like some;
I imagined it puncturing
your belly, gnawing its way up.

I couldn't do it. I dropped
the knife and everything
happened—the choking, the beating,
and the policewoman's smirk:
"You'll go back."
The last time I saw you—
handcuffed—I screamed
"You're a dead man,"
though the missing teeth
made my words impossible.

Days later, wearing a necklace
of bruised black, I purposely walked
the worst streets, hiding my mouth
behind my hand. I was 19.
Even then I knew you were moving,
surely, towards the blade.

Motel in Anchorage

I lie still, slivers of light
from the blinds dividing my body
into clean, geometric shapes.
I focus on the light, don't look
at the man getting dressed,
his ass a hairy white
planet disappearing into dirty
pants. My mouth tastes
sour and I'm sticky
and sore. Coming down
is always like this, all sharp
cornered, like the triangles
I remember from my school
math books. They were like nothing
I'd ever seen, clear and final
against the page. So different
from my home, the treeless hills
sloping to the sea.

Was I pretty, was I smart?
I don't remember.
These men are all the same,
white, black, even Eskimo.
They fuck me hard
and look the other way.
All I want is something hot
and numbing to take away their taste.
I can't go home. This city has pressed me thin
as a number—stark and unforgiving.

Mother

Now it sleeps, slug
soft and helpless.
I feel nothing.
Flesh like underdone
dough, it's a mistake,
an ugly scrap someone
tossed my way. It cries
for hours—the radio drowns
its hiccoughing sobs.
Or I shake it
until it stops, head bobbing
like a tugged balloon.

From the floor I saw
a broken bottle, a cigarette
butt, my hair—torn curtain
of matted blood and booze.
Then his boots
as he looked at me,
helpless. *Bitch*. My name.
I covered my face,
my belly unprotected,
and the boot slammed in
pain like a mirror
shattering. Even this
his son survived.

It opens its eyes, unfocused
blue. Innocent. Maybe.
Bud between fat legs proves
he's his father's son.
He'll tear me too, make me
bleed. He already has.

Pillow descends. Avenging
angel.

The Drivers

You saw me, circled back,
your blue Camaro slowing
in a predatory dance.
Coaxed into the passenger seat,
I was impressed
by the car, your mustache.
You turned on
the radio, got me high—
so high I watched
like a small, hovering bird
as you took off my clothes
in that cramped backseat.

I didn't want you,
but at 17, I didn't know
how to say that.
Later, my hands shook
as I held the phone, inventing
a jealous boyfriend. You asked
if I was alone.

Appearing at my house, anger
pumping through a vein
in your neck, you knocked
the phone I reached for
out of my hands. *Little girl,
I'm no one-night stand.*
Forcing me to the bed,
you ripped down my shorts, unzipped
your fly. Staring at my floral
wallpaper, I saw each
orange petal, sharp
and distinct as edges
of broken glass.

You called me baby
when you came, kissed
me on the mouth.
I closed my eyes,
like I sometimes still do,
afraid of your face, descending.
Years have erased
your name, still I know you,
know all your brothers.
I smile, teeth like nails,
and draw you in.

The Women in My Family

The women in my family
are strong as trees that bend
beneath a heavy snow,
bend low, branches freezing in ice
and mud, bend so far
they can't bounce back and
are trampled like weeds.
But still alive. Enduring.
Enduring unimaginable things
or maybe just a life so goddamn
lonely they begin to doubt
their own existence. My grandmother,
educated in Paris, wanted to be
a designer, but went home bent
before her father's imperious
will. She married to spite him—
took on my grandfather's motherless
girls, frightened and fierce
as two cornered kittens.
At sixty, she took me too,
though she was already slipping
into her surreptitious waltz
with an early death.
And my mother, why
I've seen her claw
at a man's legs from the floor
where he threw her, crying please
don't leave me, her words piercing
as a handful of tiny knives.

And so,
would it surprise you
if I was like them?
I'm not. Christ, I don't even

sway in a breeze. I'd rather
break with a sharp crack, a spruce exploding
in a cold snap.
My mother says, "You're so hard
hearted, so cruel, but who knows?
Maybe men want that—
a real bitch." I shrug.
I act on instinct: fast
and indifferent
as the rattlesnake hidden
beneath the fallen tree.

Manley Hot Springs, Alaska: 1975

Independence Day, and I am twelve,
dark hair falling straight, held back
by a blue bandana. My mother rents a room—
above the lodge's bar—and all night, voices rise
in slurred shouts, while outside,
gunfire rends the air in lieu of fireworks.
From the car, our dog's furious barking.
Darkness never comes; the sun doesn't set.

At five, a gunshot in the bar
then shuddering silence.
My mother shifts in her bed. "The dog,"
she says, and I dutifully go to tend her.
Quiet echoes as I edge down narrow stairs.

On the landing, a bearded man and a rifle
aimed angrily at my face.
"I thought I told all you fucking Indians
to get out of my bar."
My legs shake, wanting to run,
all I can think of is the dog
already maybe peeing on the car's seat;
when I open my mouth, words
rush out with tears—my mom and vacation
and the dog. He doesn't lower the gun,
but opens the door, shoves me out
onto the morning's cool grass.

And I am only twelve. I have never seen
a gun before. I have come from California
where night follows day in orderly fashion,
where on the Fourth of July I whirl dizzily
with sparklers in both hands, and place black pellets
on the sidewalk to see them transform
into charcoal snakes. I squeeze my eyes shut,
wish hard for some magic to take me home,

but when I open them, I see only
the unfamiliar spruce, and revelers
swaying unsteadily by. I take the dog
for a walk—I don't know what else to do.

Two young men, Indian, black hair held back
with bandanas like mine, say hello;
I gaze at my feet, whisper a reply.
In the lodge window, I see the gun's
slim shadow, so I crouch by the car
arms tight around the dog's neck, until
she pulls away, shakes herself and stretches.
There is nowhere to go but back.

I try to make myself small,
inoffensive, invisible, but that man
grabs my shoulder hard then lets me go,
rifle still dangling from one hand, an evil
appendage. Cringing like a beat dog, I leap
for the stairs, imagining the rifle raising,
the furious noise, and a sudden sharp
crack in my back.

Hours later, my mother
sends me to breakfast while she searches out
the lodge owner. Her voice rises
from another room like bursts of gunfire.
I mop syrup around my plate
with a scrap of blueberry pancake,
stomach tight. The bearded man comes in,
stares hard at me. "She looks like a goddamn Native."
The other diners nod, and I hang
my head, face burning.

Night Crossing

You feel the ferry glide
over the shadowed river.
The car you sit in seems
to slide sideways, out
of control, unsettling

as earlier, in the bar
when twenty-five years
of living in one world
was torn away,
when the white paint
stripped from your face
revealed the truth:
You are not one of them.
"The only good Indian
is a dead. . ."
the voice said, too
loud, and you looked up,
thinking it a joke.
The hatred in the man's
eyes was real,
and it was meant for you.
Suddenly, you understood
the stares, the looking through
as if you were no more
substantial than chill
night air. Words tossed
over a white man's shoulder
burrowed into your flesh
like ticks.

You turn away
from the town, as the ferry,
current–caught, skids
to the far shore. The darkness
is so solid, your eyes strain
to see. Then you drive
into the night, a barely
tolerated visitor
on the lighted shore.

II

Twilight at Twenty–Nine Below

Love in Autumn

I am in love again
and the wind rushes
through the trees—
a snake gliding beneath fallen
leaves. I am moved
by small things:
the hair on your forearms
curling golden
as kestrel feathers, your voice
a trilling weight
in my ears. You
look away from me
afraid of this passion
curving my hands into
sickles.

Wanting You

I feel your shoulders
shift, fragile as a falcon's
wings, feel you shiver
from the midsummer chill, from desire.
You kiss me. Your teeth
are even white bones behind your lips;
your tongue burns in my mouth—
not fire, but ice, a finger
of frost chipped from a glacier.
Everything becomes sharp,
clear, as on those cold nights
when each star is etched
against the winter sky.
Your eyes are crowberries
growing on treeless summits,
dark as the winter solstice,
dark as night pooling
into footprints in the snow.
I lay my cheek against
your chest—smooth field
of polished glass—hear your blood
chase itself through your body;
it hums like a high-tension wire.
I want to see inside you:
the secret spring of your heart,
the bones buried beneath
ridges of muscle, the marrow
like veins of ore in stone.
I lift your hand to my lips,
trying to erase the fine lines
flowing across the plain of your palm,
trying to erase the edges
of doubt in your mind,
trying to erase everything
except you and me
and this pure, blue burning night.

Anima, Animus

Struggling beneath the weight
of sleep, I feel your body hover
over mine, light as the shadow
of cloud. Only a dream, still my body
knows yours, yearns for it,
as a snake must sometimes yearn
for the limbs it lacks.
Waking, I remember
muscles taut under their sheath
of skin, the way our bodies rocked,
desolate with longing.
At night your bones
migrate into my flesh, leaving
our faces indistinguishable.
So we continue—tangled—
waiting for the fiery animals
to rise from their still sea,
burning us, gnawing us free.

The Poet Surveys the Wreckage of Her Life

These are the things in her house:
A box full of bootleg tapes.
A tub of dogfood and two pink
plastic dishes. Five empty
beer bottles. A bowl full of change.
Half a pot of coffee—cold. A wedding ring,
no longer worn. A single
sapphire earring. Piles of papers.
A coyote skull. Two ivory birds.
Handfuls of bullets—9mm.
Books. A cashmere coat.
A gin bottle full of pennies.
A bag of her last lover's clothes. His mail.
A VCR. A broken black
and white TV. A pack of cigarettes
left by the second to the last lover,
the drunken one who still comes around.
A bed of sleeping bags and foam pads.
The quilt sewn by a friend. A pair
of her ex-husband's underwear. The torn
T-shirt she sleeps in, left by the last lover,
the one who matters.
The smell of his absence.
The painkillers she takes sometimes
to sleep. The loaded pistol
by the bed. A picture of her
in her last lover's arms.
And everywhere, her own desire
for release, bright as the flame
on the propane stove.

Twilight at Twenty-Nine Below

and again you say
you are leaving. Out there
ice fog obscures
street signs, intentions,
as your voice—
blue bottles breaking—
belies the careful calm
of words. You say
it can't be
any other way. Meaning
skids off; I'm left
behind, heart too
turgid to evoke
emotion. The streets
are frozen.
The streets are frozen.
Fast fading light.
No sure path back.

Winter Storms

for John

In the Arctic, the sea freezes
three feet down, trapping
all life beneath it. Here,
it is possible to walk
on water, head bowed
before the dark, winter storms.
But for me, the only miracle
is memory: you and I drifting

in the clear currents
of a tropical sea.
Or the view from our hotel:
an iguana grey as old
cement, sleeping on the worn
slats of an open window;
the sea—a turquoise
tile—burning beneath
the midday sun. And you appearing
on the beach, legs pale
as sand, a Neptune
with fins and snorkel.

If we could return
to that place, I would.
But it seems long ago
and out of reach. Each night,
I dream uneasily of ships
bound in ice, and below them
I see the ocean floor
is littered with the luminous
bones of whales.

Detail, Final Scene

Midwinter and the stars
burn in their places,
those cold bodies
we wish upon. Twists
of ice in your beard,
frost flowering from
your mouth as you speak,
the words tangible
in air. Notice
the black spruce—
uneasy fingers reaching
for an indifferent sky.
And the shadows,
lengthening between us.

Young Widow Walking Home

Her shift ends just past 3 a.m.,
so she shucks the skirt
for a pair of wool pants,
tucks her tips away
and heads home. Some nights
she's drunk, but she always walks
alone. Other waitresses worry,
offer rides, but she looks
past them, faint shadows on a wall.

When she drinks, she thinks of nothing
more than scrunch of boots
in snow. Tonight, her mind leaps—
a restive dog on a leash.
She gazes at two birch, bent
close to breaking—an early snow caught
in their net of leaves. She wonders if
they'll survive 'til spring.
She thinks of her cold cabin,
the wood stove she'll fire up,
the bottle of brandy
by the bed. His hands.
His hands on the ax
last spring: swing, arc,
birch split clean.

A car glides by. Tail lights flash.
She's not afraid. Too many nights
she teases his loaded .44, tongue
lingering on the muzzle,
nudging the barrel
against the roof of her mouth.
She sleeps in his clothes.
He's been gone nine months, long enough

to have the baby they never conceived.
She thinks of it again,
him under the car, one toe poking
from his torn tennis shoe, the jack shifting—
no time for a scream—transmission crushing
his chest like an egg.
Like an egg, she thinks, his ribs
an ivory shell and his blood vivid
as the broken yolk.

Around the cabin, birch twist
into a snarl of bent trunks,
broken branches. She knows
she exists like them:
mute and unexpectant.

Autumn Equinox

You don't mention
love. Instead
you write of home:
birch rattling bare
limbs, puddles rimmed
in ice, children discarding
crayoned cornucopias
on the stiffening earth.
You tell me the geese
have long fled south—in days
you will follow.
*I may even make it
your way by spring.*
You say you miss me.
I'm sorry. Your face
is already indistinct,
an image glimpsed
through frosted glass.

Of Ivy and a Plum Tree

Ivy covers the yard, glossy
and luxuriant, choking out all
other vegetation. It hides
its secrets: beetles, black widows,
and those other spiders—long and pale
as the calla lily the ivy slowly
swallows. Like the men
my mother brings home, defects
hidden by their beguiling smiles.
My mother, still very young, tries
to manage them as she does
the ivy—trimming here, training
a vine into position,
but the heart–shaped leaves
are always triumphant.
Firm in her hopes, she digs up
a great swath. Here she plants
a plum tree, slender and feminine
in its garment of purple foliage.
She longs to see it bloom,
pale sweetness balancing the bruise
of leaves. But it does not.
Three years it exists, refusing
to flourish, a stubborn
exile amidst the ivy.
Finally she gives up,
lets the vines encroach, 'til the tree,
no taller but still forcing out
its few dark leaves, founders
and is forgotten.

Years later, my mother—
still unmarried—is no longer sure
of her own grace. Each day she grows
more fragile, loneliness blooming
beneath her eyes in lavender
shadows. Returning to that house
we left long ago, I see
it is all gone—ivy torn
from its bed, tree uprooted.
Only bare ground remains,
raw and unstruggling.

The Unridden Horses

A deep claw foot tub,
a wavering slant
of late afternoon light,
wildflowers wilting in a chipped
glass jar, and his touch—
turned tentative and unfamiliar.
Outside the narrow window
there were horses.

She recalls these images, carries
them like talismans, fragile
beads of days viewed in a dim
archival light. That was their last
trip together, the two of them
quiet, gentle with one another,
like long separated siblings
no longer certain
of their shared past.
Just ahead, they sensed
their separate futures: restive
as the unridden horses.

Clean Sheets

Next door a woman is hanging
wet sheets on a line. Billowing
and snapping, tongues of clouds
fallen to earth, I try to understand
their language, but the whiteness
rebukes me. Today,
your letter came. I will say
it doesn't matter, but these sheets—flags
of cloth too pure for any
lover—seem enormous, an empty
page I cannot fill.

Rain at the State Line

Driving out of the storm,
a momentary break in the clouds
and the cab of the truck
floods with sun, the low hills
like a yellow dog sleeping.
Before them, black clouds
and a fringe of rain
like hair hiding the face
of someone loved but unknown.
The light is a temporary grace.
She thinks of the fragility
of time, how this moment, already
encased in the amber of memory,
is changing into something brittle
and precious. Together they ride
quietly through waves of light,
an ease between them
she senses they will not know
again. They will meet the rain
at the state line, drive into it,
sadness settling on them
like an old coat. She feels
something irrevocable passing,
the quiet ache of loss
for something not yet gone.
Years later, she remembers
the drive, notes the symptoms
of what was still to come.
She sees the two of them
as innocents, approaching rain.

III

At the Sorbonne

In memory of my grandmother:
Grace Stretcher Sedwarft
1907–1969

At the Sorbonne, 1925

Not spring, but fall,
still it was Paris—the air
chill and effervescent
as champagne I tasted
for the first time that day.
Everything was fashion: the sky
a bolt of good blue wool,
autumn leaves appliqued
in gold lamé. Sent to study
literature, I drafted
dress designs in the borders
of my notebooks, lingered near
the fashion houses, hoping
for a glimpse of the great
couturiers: Poiret, Fortuny,
Chanel. So secretive, schoolmates
thought I had a lover,
yet there was no love but this:
the feel of cloth in my hands—
yards of washed silk, Egyptian cotton,
fine merino wool. That afternoon
I could see my future
draped before me, a pattern
to be stitched.

L'Heure Bleue

Dusk, and the cafes
begin to fill, but I
turn towards the park
drifting away from the tinkle
of glassware and women's
laughter. The blue hour,
they call it, and I understand
why as the sky's color deepens.
I pass couples huddled on benches,
lingering along the shadowy paths,
but I'm glad to be alone.
A lover would distract me
from the pattern of leaves
against the bruised light.
This beauty makes me tremble.
Suddenly, the sky is a skirt,
deep sapphire peau de soie
overlaid with lace—Chantilly, yes,
but black, not white, suggesting
leaves against the evening
sky. And a sequined bodice,
perhaps, bringing to mind
the night's first stars.
Or is that too much?
I hurry home to my sketchbook,
eager to resurrect the hour's
drama in a different design.

The Unveiling of the Paris Collections, 1926

Two days before I left home,
Father and I watched our penned
pheasants scratch in the dirt.
We named you Grace, he said, *hoping
you would be beautiful. But you're
plain as those pheasant hens.*
He laughed, lit his pipe.
When I turned away, he caught
my arm. *You'll never marry.*
His hair was the color
of cognac, held above a flame.

No, I'm not beautiful,
but I am elegant in black
crepe de chine and Mother's
heirloom pearls. And watching
les mannequins, I know
they are only shopgirls
transformed. Look at her,
rare and fine as a jeweled ibis.
And that one, in the gown
of gas–blue beads. Her thin
figure is unwavering as a column
of clear water. They are all lovely
by design—bobbed hair
and yards of faux pearls.
Off the runway, they shed
their glamour with the clothes.
Only le couturier will be
remembered. Beauty, Father,
is better created than possessed.

In a Letter, Unsent

Father, today I received
your letter. It is May;
Paris is clothed in new
spring shades, the flowers
fanciful as embroidered
dragons. You wouldn't care.
I begged to stay,
but all you can see for me
is the dark severity
of the schoolroom or library.
Talent means nothing
when constrained by a woman's
flesh. You say I am
a disgrace, that you will send
no more money. Father, I'm staying.
I will sell my books,
my clothes. Mother's pearls
will pay the rent.
I'll take in piece-work:
stitch beads and sequins on flappers'
gowns. There's a woman designer here
who takes girls like me—
girls with promise—as apprentices.
I'll go to her.

Writing this, I still recall
how casually you killed
our pheasants for the table—
snapping their necks with practiced
hands. My future is not
yours to take.

The Wilson Elementary School

In the end, I went,
boarded the train leaving
Paris, the train that led
to the ship that steamed
me home. My father's money
retreated like a wave,
dragging me back—drowning—
across the Atlantic.
Talent alone was not enough
to buoy me up; I watched
my future founder
when I could not pay
the rent. On that final
crossing, I cried
as I watched men shoot
skeet from the ship's deck—
clay pigeons exploding
like my ambitions, shards
sinking into the sea
without a trace. My arrival
here was inevitable.

Now I stand, in a brown
wool dress of my own design,
paralyzed before the children
repeating their lessons by
rote. I can see no further
than the end of the day—
the last bell, and erasers
clapped together, chalk rising
like a tangible ghost,
the spirit of something
left behind.

IV

Winter Solstice

Reaching Destruction Bay

We arrive at one a.m., the first
day out from Fairbanks.
Beyond the frame houses
of the tiny town rests the silver
green reach of Kluane, an endless
finger crooked through rock.
On the map, it's a pinched
gate, a narrow place on the path
that leads to the exposed
crowd of the lower 48. Here,
the highway thins to a ledge
of dirt and gravel poised between
the lake and the mountain's
rock face. It has rained
for weeks. The radio reports
the road may be washed out;
still we drive forward, knowing
this the only way down.
The rain has stilled,
but the choppy lake reflects
nothing. We stop as the highway
disappears. In the sudden
silence, the lake gnaws
at the ruined road. Kluane,
swallower of ships, of souls. A roar
breaks the stillness—a D-8 Cat
appears around the curve,
shockingly yellow against
the wash of granite and green.
A shouted conversation
with the operator, a chain,
then a wrenching jolt.
We are pulled, impossibly,
into a new world.

Museum Piece: The Birdskin Parka

She made it
the spring before
she became a woman.
When she slipped it on—
skins of eider ducks
and tundra swans—
she danced, whirling
over tundra, flying
beside the grey
Bering Sea.

She died, barely twenty,
in a white man's epidemic
neither the shaman
nor the priest could cure.
The smoke from her burning
body rose higher
than soaring birds.

Her parka hangs here
between panes of glass.
Earthbound.

The Whaling Captain's Woman

At Herschel Island, the wind
shuffled against the ice-bound
ship, speaking a language
alien as your own.
I could hear it
as I sewed—evil spirits
seeking entry. I was seventeen,
already a widow, and I cursed
my hand—too skilled
with a needle—as I stitched
your boots, your parka.
At night, you took me
to your bed; still I dreamed
of my own husband
his face worn smooth
as ivory by death.

There were four of us,
women without husbands,
brought aboard at Point Hope
to sew. I cried
when you dropped us
off hundreds of miles
from our home, but I did not
cry for you. That summer
I gave birth to a boy
with sea-colored eyes.

Now I am married
to a Teller man; he brings
us meat and teaches the boy
to hunt. Each year,
your ship returns, its sails
swallowing the sun. You want
the boy. He is Eskimo.
He will never be yours.

Flight of Swans

One day in late summer
I saw Raven walking along
the river. He was disguised
as Old Man Solomon—wearing
loose trousers and beaded
boots—but I wasn't fooled.
I followed him to the cutbank
where my brother trapped muskrat
last winter. Raven stepped off
the bank and disappeared in a swirl
of water. When I told Papa
he said I should be
a shaman. Mama told him
that time was past, and sent me
to the mission school instead.
They spoke English there;
its silver metal and sharp
edges hurt my ears.
Once when the choir sang,
I saw angels. White and fierce
as tundra swans, their wings
beat the air around me.
I told everyone about them—
if I couldn't be a shaman
I would be a saint.
When Sister Superior heard,
she slapped me hard.
I didn't say anything.
Out the window, I saw angels
settling on the pond.

France, 1348

My master had a gyrfalcon;
a wedding gift from a northern
lord, she was radiant
and white as my lady's
bridal gown. I was more attentive
to her than to all the other birds.
I lived in the mews,
heard her bells in sleep,
and my teeth clenched to tighten
her hood in my dreams.

One afternoon in August
as the falcon began
her stoop, I saw a man
ride towards the manor
on a white-lathered horse.
The gyrfalcon cried
as she brought down the prey;
I turned to attend her.
From the partridge I cut
the falcon's share, and stood transfixed
as her beak, a graceful sickle,
tore the bird's flesh.
Returning, we passed the stable,
saw the messenger tending his horse.
He was pale and coughed blood.

He died that night,
my master and his lady
three days later. Wracked
with coughs and chills,
I hobbled to the mews,
unhooded the birds
and carried them out.
Confused, but hungry,

they took to the sky.
I removed the bells
and jesses from the gyrfalcon
last, my fingers clumsy
with sorrow. She was used
to me and would not rouse.
Hunger finally drove her off
and I held her hood
tight to my face
as I watched her spiral slowly
against the morning sky.

My Mother's Wolves

pace, chained shadows,
one black, one white,
eyes the color of stones
unknown to man.
They pace and crouch,
uneasy as wind, confined
in the ashes
of the city, where feral children
prowl the empty streets,
building bonfires, carrying
daggers of flame.

My mother's wolves
are shy and trembling, unused
to smoke and steel
and the clattering cries
of this place.
If she let them go,
they'd streak through
the winter night, pure light
and pure shadow, side by side
ascending the sky.
And their howls
would shatter the moon, unleashing
torrents of quicksilver
stars, till even the fierce infants
would be baptized
in a corona of wolf–light.

Fetish

I give to you
an onyx bear.
This bear brings
dreams in his teeth
night visions—shimmering
tatters that trail
like aurora across
the sparking sky.
Dream bear sleeps
underground where trees
are fists of roots
clenched against
ice. Underground
in the dark womb
coal foxes chase
one another, bursting
into brilliant blue
beads of flame.
Here the wind
is black with an edge
of shattered glass
or ice grown dangerous
during sun's long sleep.
The wind reaps change
and bear is reborn
wading across the blood
black river, shaggy
and certain beneath
an ever eclipsing moon.
All this I would
give to you.

Seawater and Stinging Nettles

Twenty–two below, you stand
pissing off the porch
in a wolverine–trim parka
and tennis shoes. Cold
pimples your bare thighs.
You flick away your cigarette,
red arc in the darkness. Step inside.
Shiver. Shuck the shoes
and coat. Come here.
I'm waiting.
You grin, drain the rest
of the vodka, a volley of comets
unleashed in your throat.

You're crazy drunk. I don't care.
I fuel you with my body—
blood and bones distilled
to the purest liquor.
You say I taste of seawater
and stinging nettles, that familiar
and that sharp.
And I laugh, light flashing
behind my closed eyes, a handful of stars
rising into new constellations.

The Perfecting of Desire

This is what matters:
the curve of muscle
in his forearm, the way
he smells—smoke, old leather,
beer. What matters
is desire, the way
his beard rubs my thigh,
the way my breath stops
as he slides inside me.
Our flesh sighs into light,
into flame, darkness illuminate.
Stripped down to the porous
skeleton of necessity, we are refined
to pure male and pure female, encompassed
by forces larger than ourselves.
My teeth graze his neck;
his hands bruise my shoulders.
And when we come
to ourselves, slightly sheepish, strangers
in our own bodies, we do not speak
of the place we left.
Some nights, we surrender
like angels, shaky and awed
by what we can do.

Every Day She Bathes in the Sea

the waves lapping at her
like hungry mouths. She remembers
the first man, how he parted
her thighs with teeth and tongue,
how he left a bit of his hardness
wedged within her.
Each one added to it,
until her stomach grew firm
and translucent as a ball of amber.

At night her full belly glows.
The men come, sniffing and pressing;
she lets them take her
behind the sea–wall and hibiscus.
First only the handsome waiter,
then others: a laborer with bad teeth,
a boy thin as a blade
of grass. Entering her, they become
intangible as air, leaving her free
to think of the ocean: spirals
of tiny fish, barracuda still
as swords beneath the waves.

The amber grows heavier each day.
She imagines walking barefoot
across the burning coral, waves sucking
at her calves, her thighs.
She knows how water loosens
the skin, imagines it peeling
away like petals falling
from a rose. The current
will expose the black flapping thing
inside her, let the lump of amber
drop in a single, painless spasm.
Freed finally from the net
of bone and skin, she will glide
like the manta ray—
dark and fantastic.

Wild Horses

I remember
when I was fourteen
and Papa caught me
sneaking out to meet
that hot–blooded ranch hand
from Pine Lake.

He beat me good.
Said he was beating out
my wild Indian blood.
Mama never said a word
but watched him
with dark berry eyes.
Papa told me
Louisa, a woman
has two choices
in this world—
wife or whore.
You had best
remember that.

My sister Charlotte
dreamed of being a wife
from the time she could
walk. She married a white man,
had three babies
in four years.

And I dreamed
of wild horses.

I remember
what it felt like
to be young
to be as fresh
and new as green wood.
I remember
riding my pony across
hot summer fields
with strangers and coming
back with lovers.

I loved white boys.
Tom, the ranch hand
had hair as fair
as winter wheat.
At eighteen, he was half
man, half boy.
His arms were smooth
as river stones.

I loved Indian boys
who smelled of rain
and woodsmoke.
I remember
that Archambault boy.
He brought me gifts
of wild geese
and venison.

I married
a Blackfoot man
whose skin was warm
and brown as the earth
we lived on. I loved
the way he smelled—
clean and wild
as a young horse.

Now I am alone.
I sit by my stove
drinking coffee
with three sugars
and baking pies
for my grandchildren.
And I laugh.
I laugh because
Papa was wrong.
No one cares
what I was like then.
No one else remembers.

After Raven Hall

for Diana

That favored evening, light spilled
from the sky, bright and fine
as strands of your baby's hair.
Rain quieted; the air smelled
green and grey—woods and wet
pavement. We stepped from the shadow
of the porch to the cut-crystal
gleam of sun and water. From a puddle,
movement—a frog, rare this far north.
In an instant, we shed our years,
became little girls: chasing, crouching
and leaping after. Captured,
the frog's heart beat hard
against the palm of my hand.
Leopard spots of mud green,
a belly pale as mint candy,
we stroked gently, let it go.

All afternoon, we'd talked
of our lives: pain addressed
obliquely as wild animals glimpsed
through the forest's growth.
Driving home, all that
put aside, we spoke
of old Native stories,
how wealth woman took
the shape of a frog. I smiled,
wondered when our wealth
would appear.

Years later, I understood.
Her ways are unforeseen,
yet she comes, bearing ordinary
mysteries: sunlight after storm,
and the unexpected pleasure
of a frog, resting like a gold piece
on the palm of one hand.

Approaching the Winter Solstice

In Alaska, your nights bleed
into each other, the sun
a shiver of grey
above the horizon at noon.
Here, with seasons shifting
almost imperceptibly, I close
my eyes against a vast expanse
of sage and mesquite, dream
of you, of blue shadows
in the afternoons, of snow
crusting dwarf black spruce.
Since I've gone do you notice
the birch pearled in ice,
or the ptarmigan rising
like blizzards from the drifts:
pure mystery of white on white.

The desert allows
no such excess, but here is sweet
breath of sage, rising
wind. Its hot gusts scour
away dream, desire, then whisper
in my ear: Listen,
you are of this earth.
If I could give you one thing,
it would be this wind.
Take what is offered;
it is a gift.